TANA HOBAN

I Read Signs

Greenwillow
Books
New York

This one
is for
all my
children

*With many thanks
to all the sign-finders*

Greenwillow Books, a division of
William Morrow & Company, Inc.,
105 Madison Avenue,
New York, N.Y. 10016.
Printed in the
United States of America
First Edition
10 9 8 7 6 5 4 3 2 1

Library of Congress
Cataloging in Publication Data
Hoban, Tana.
I read signs.
Summary: Introduces signs
and symbols frequently
seen along the street.
1. Traffic signs and signals
—Juvenile literature.
2. Street signs—
Juvenile literature.
3. Signs and sign-boards—
Juvenile literature.
[1. Traffic signs and signals.
2. Street signs.
3. Signs and signboards.
4. Signs and symbols]
I. Title.
TE228.H63 1983
001.55'2   83-1482   7-12-84 BTSB 10.88
ISBN 0-688-02317-7
ISBN 0-688-02318-5 (lib. bdg.)

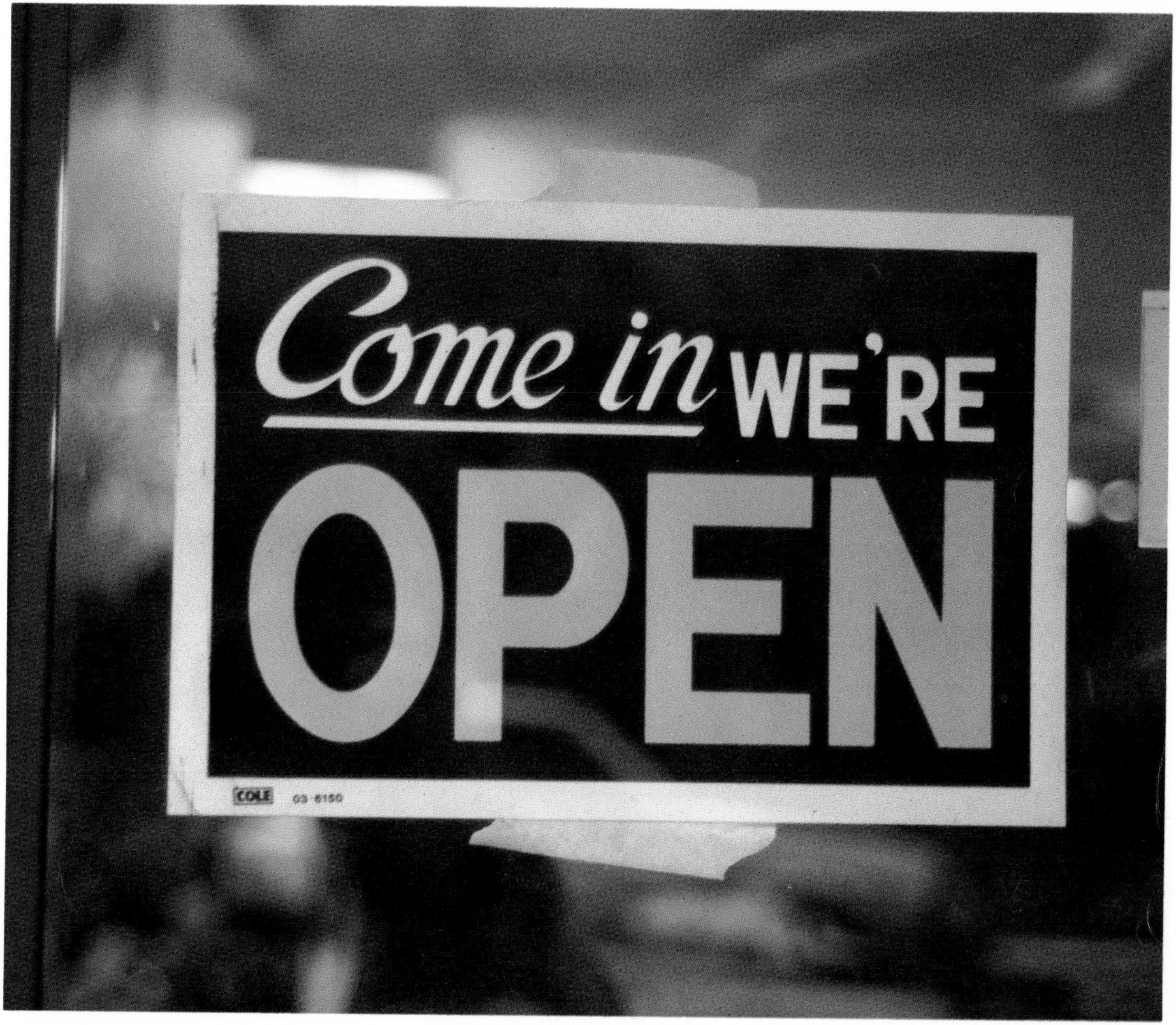
Come in WE'RE
OPEN
COLE 03-6150

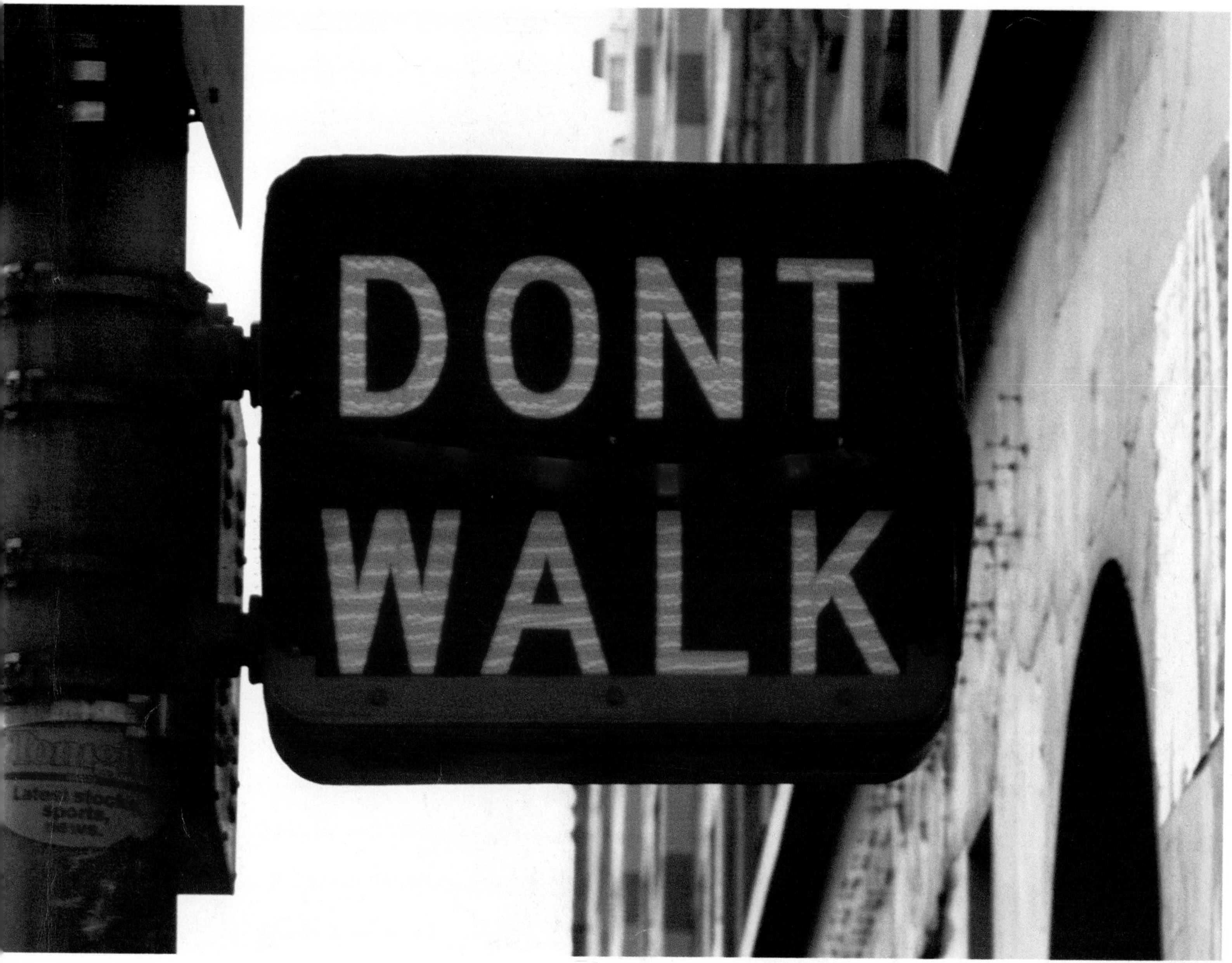
DONT
WALK

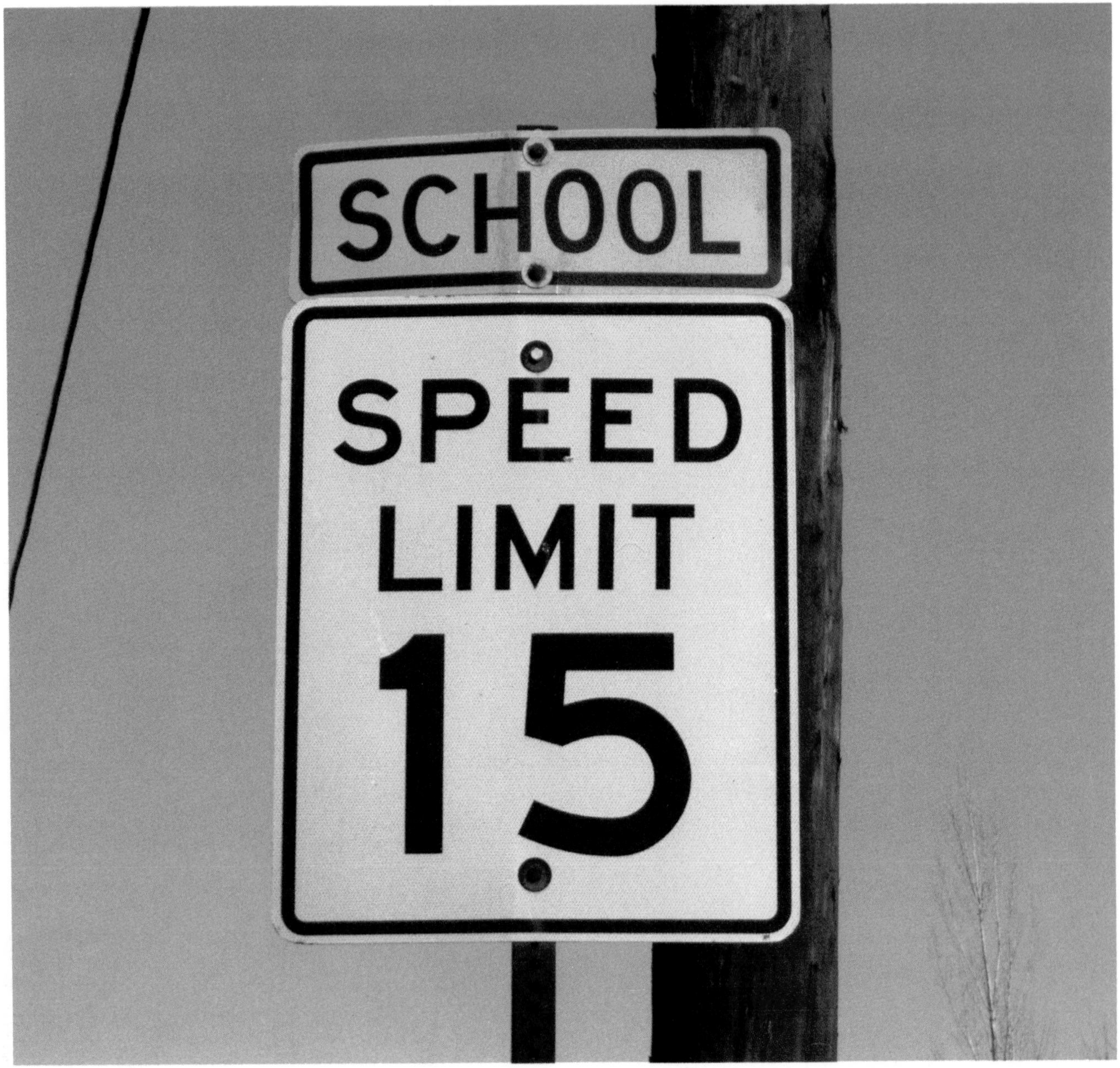
SCHOOL
SPEED
LIMIT
15

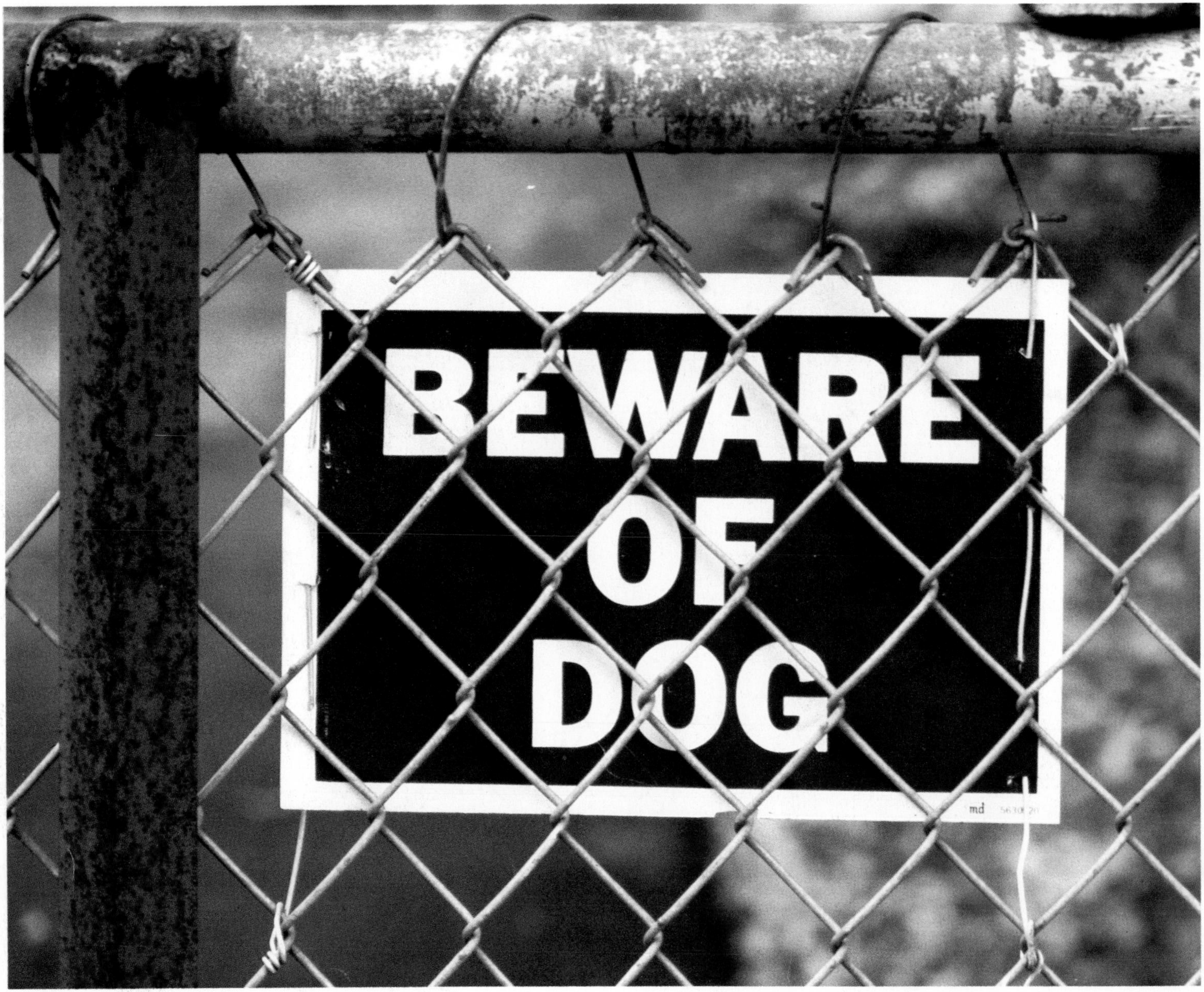
BEWARE
OF
DOG

← FIRE HOSE

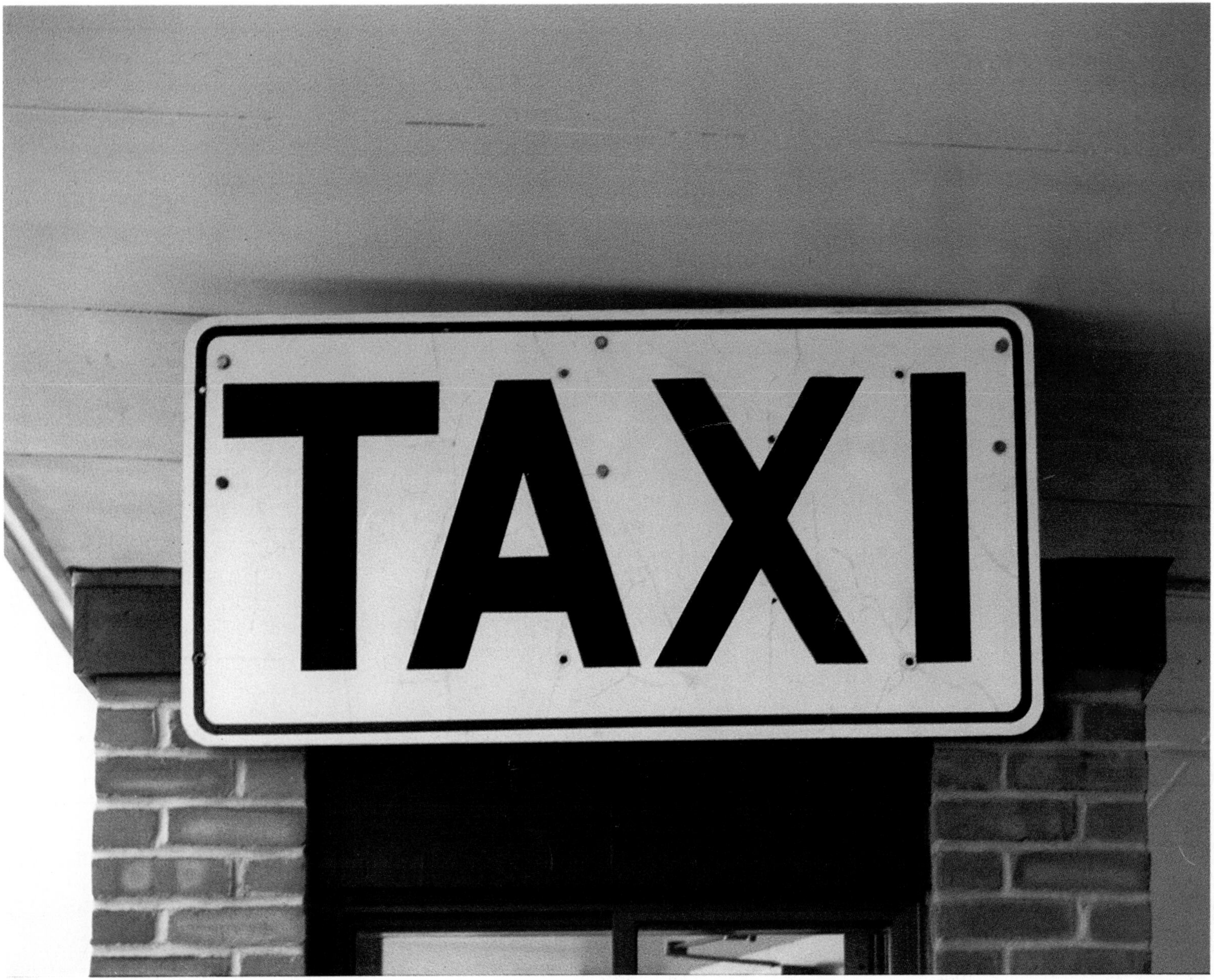
TAXI

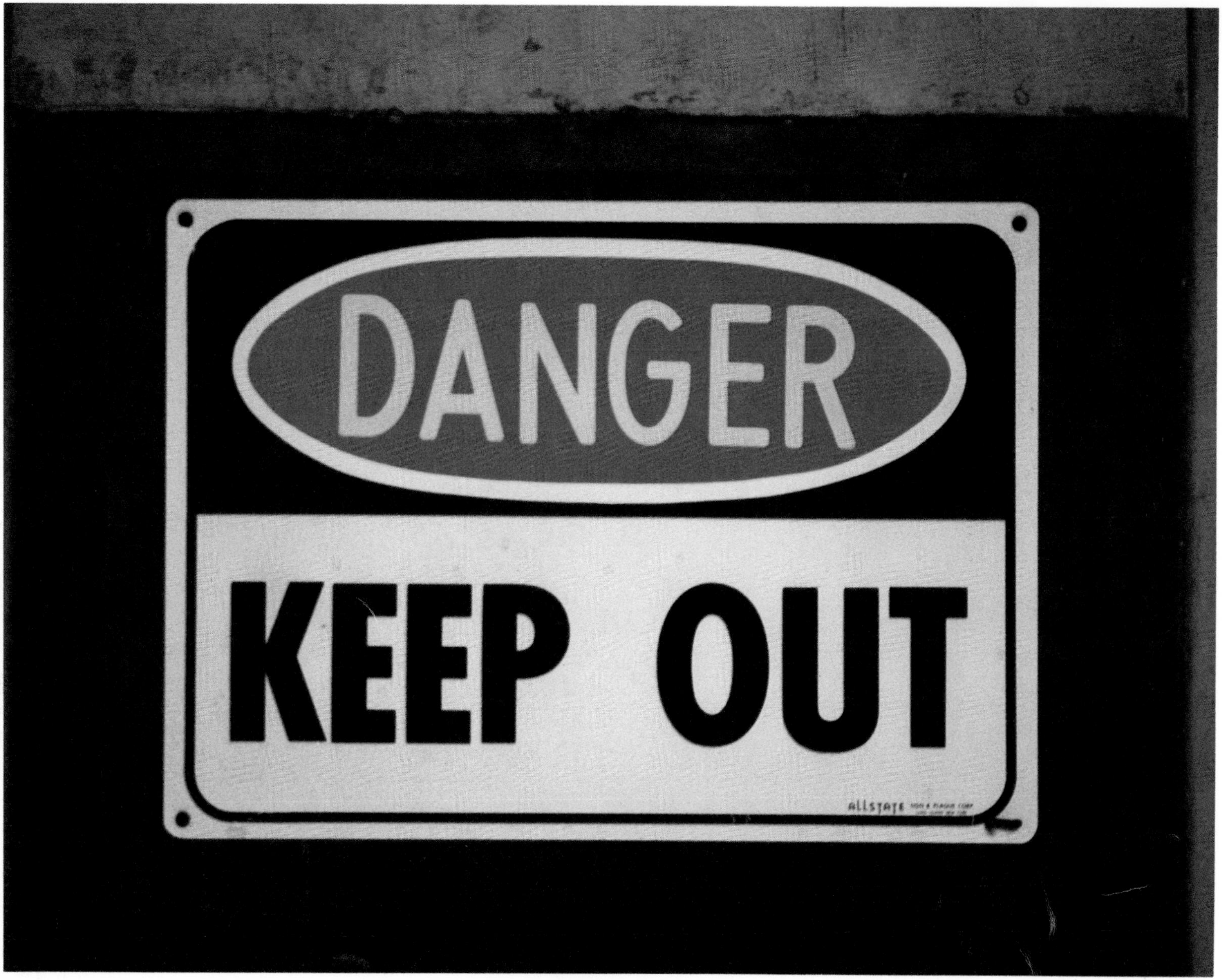
DANGER
KEEP OUT
ALLSTATE

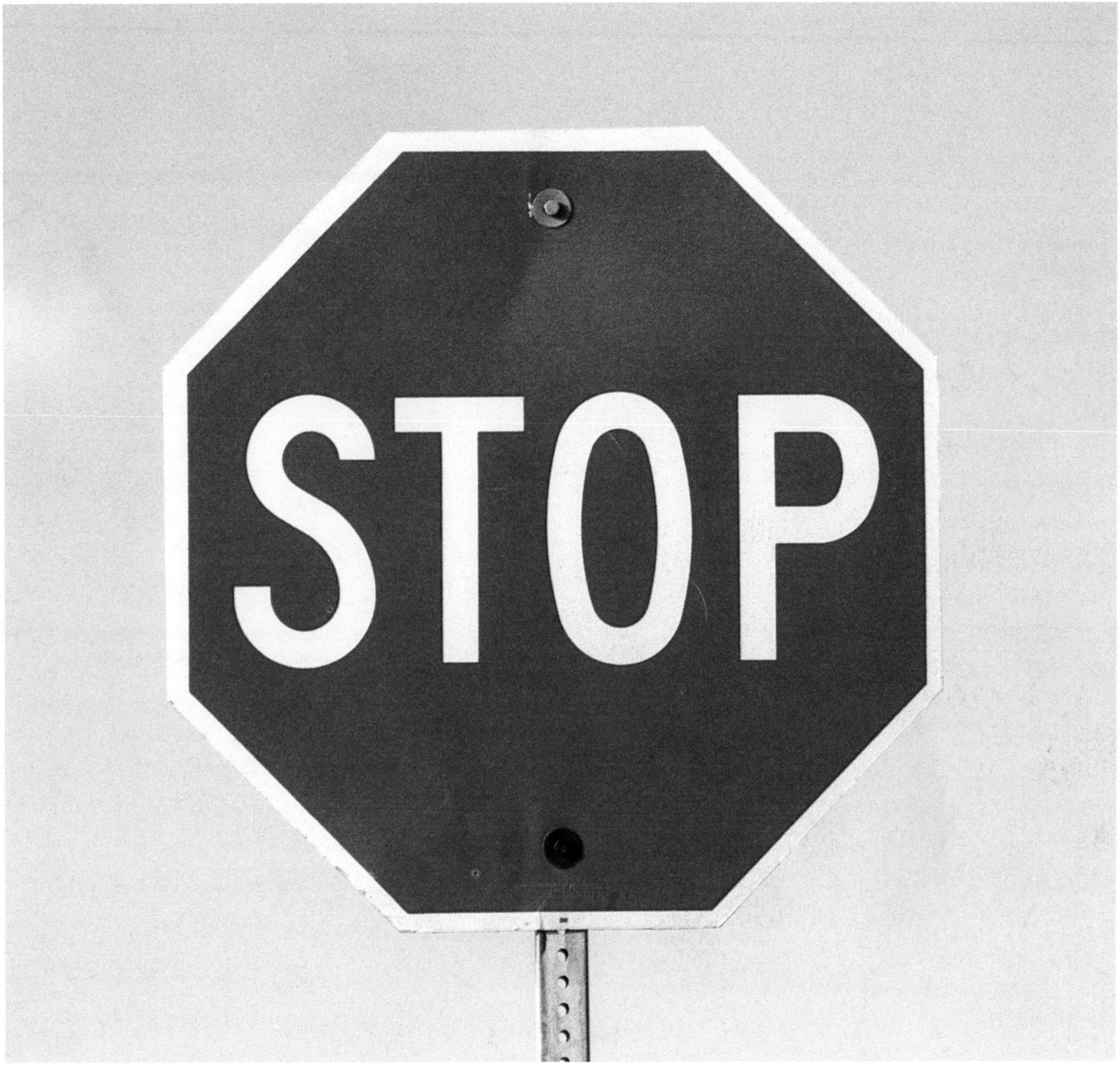
STOP

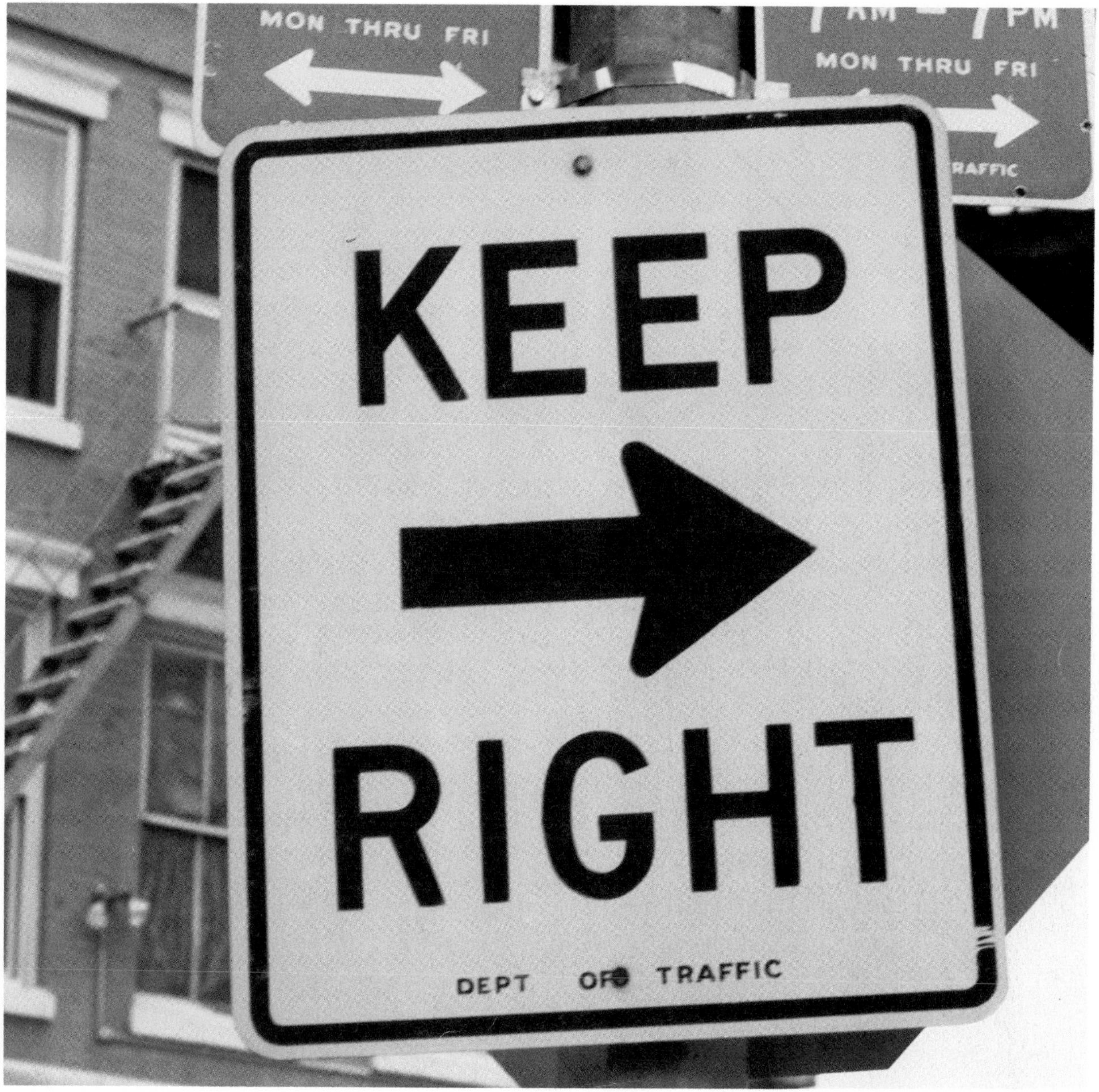
MON THRU FRI
MON THRU FRI
KEEP
RIGHT
DEPT OF TRAFFIC

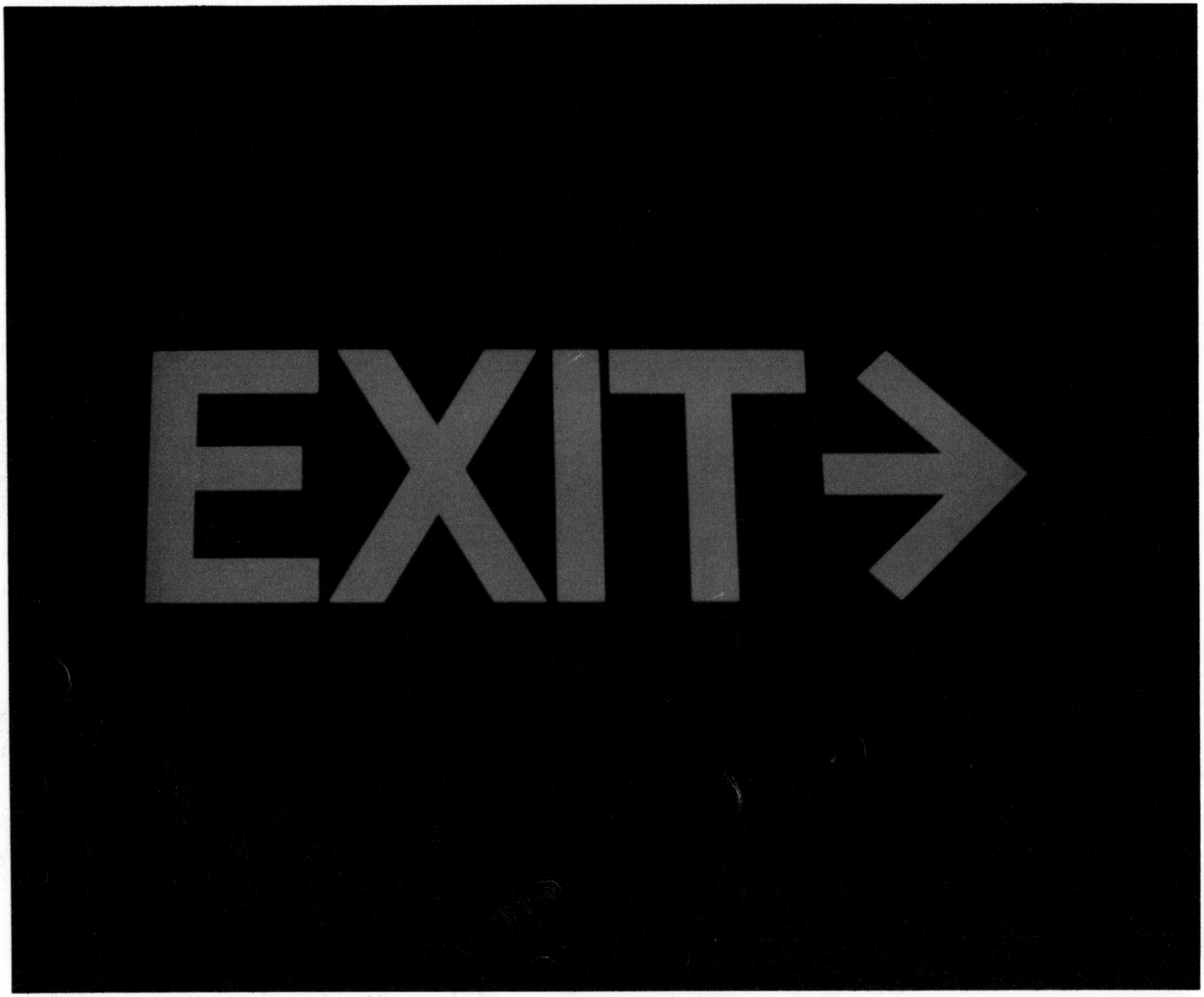
EXIT

NO STANDING

EXPRESS

DEPT OF TRANSPORTATION

CAUTION

WATCH FOR
CHILDREN

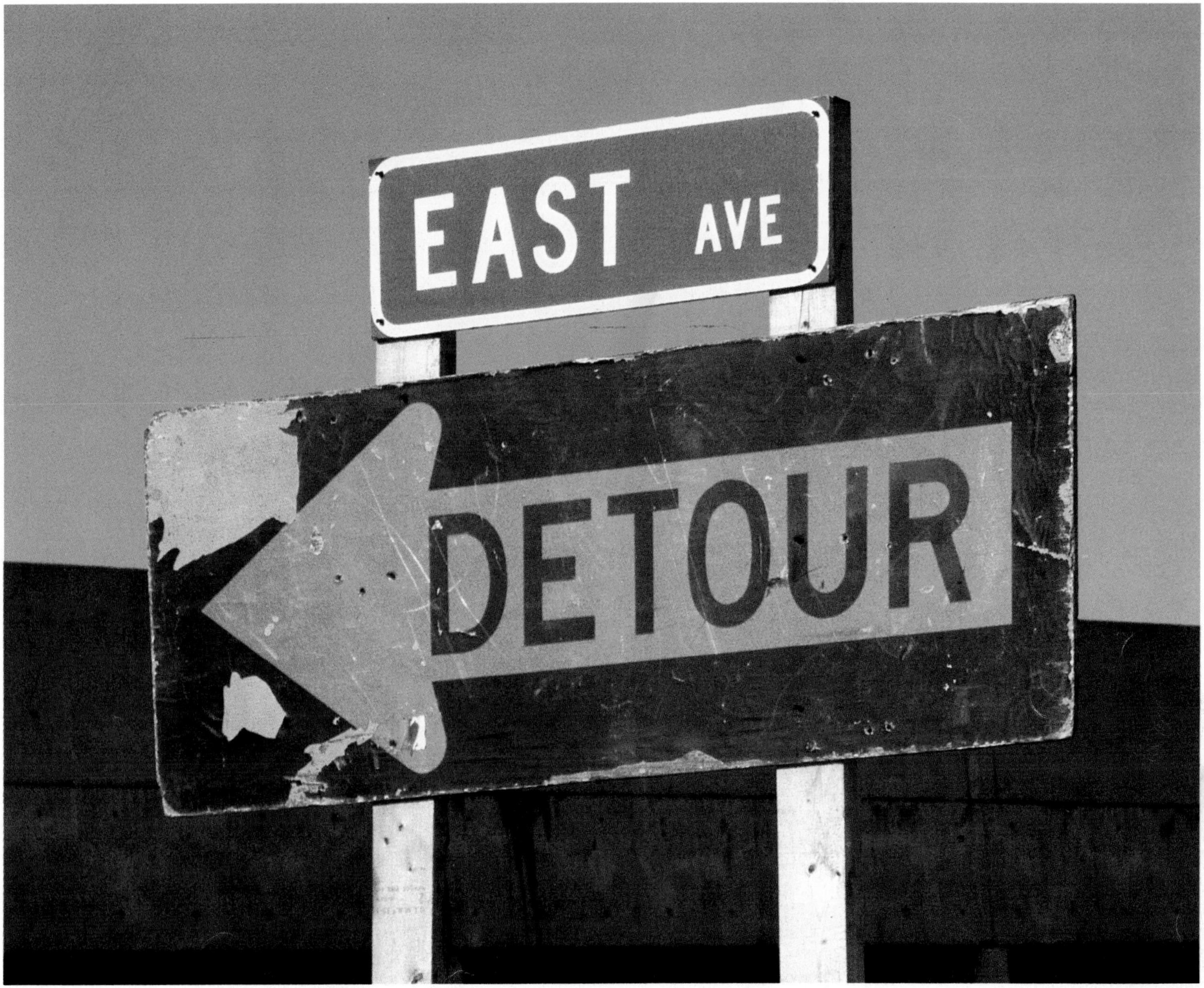
EAST AVE
DETOUR

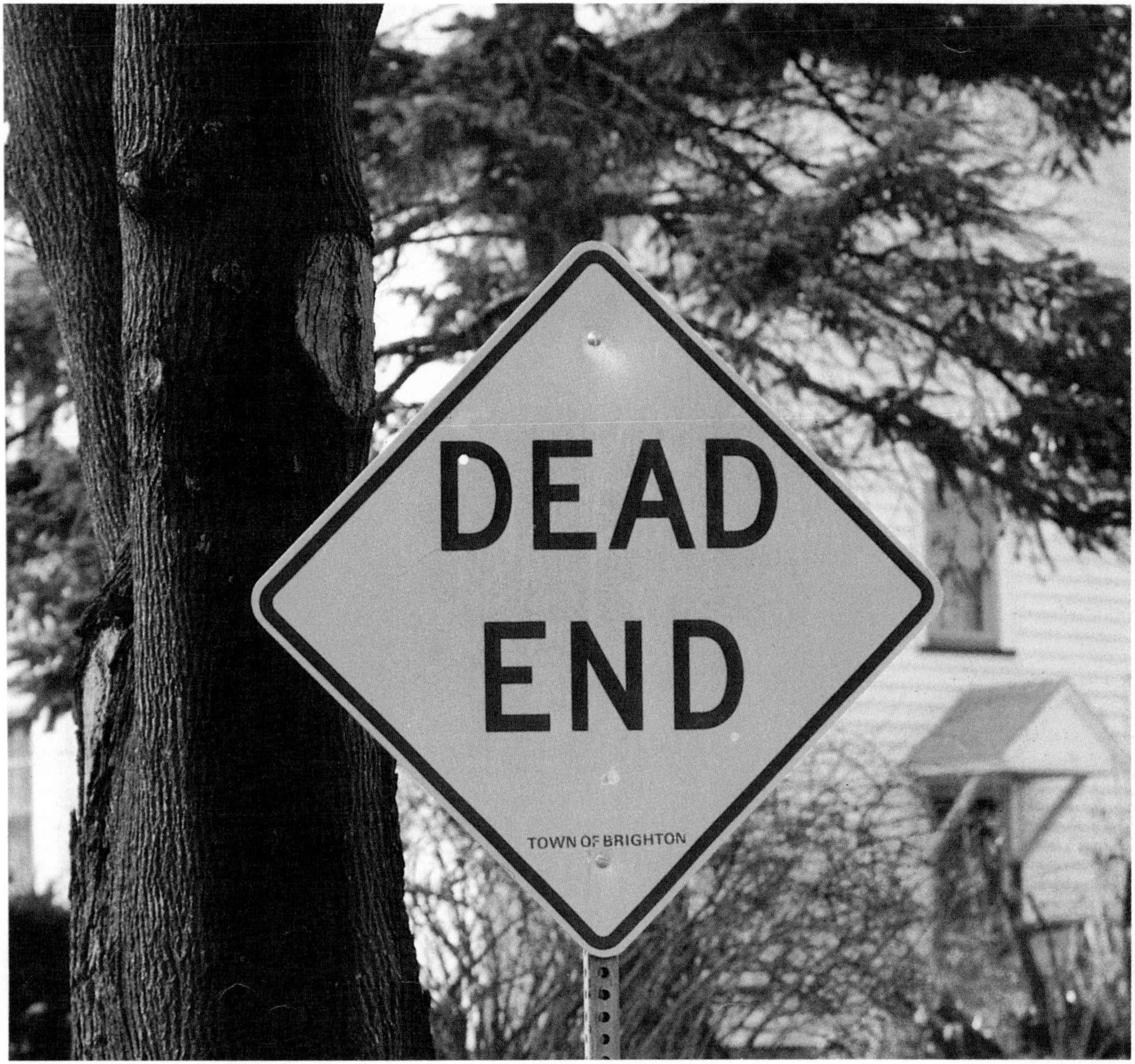
DEAD
END
TOWN OF BRIGHTON

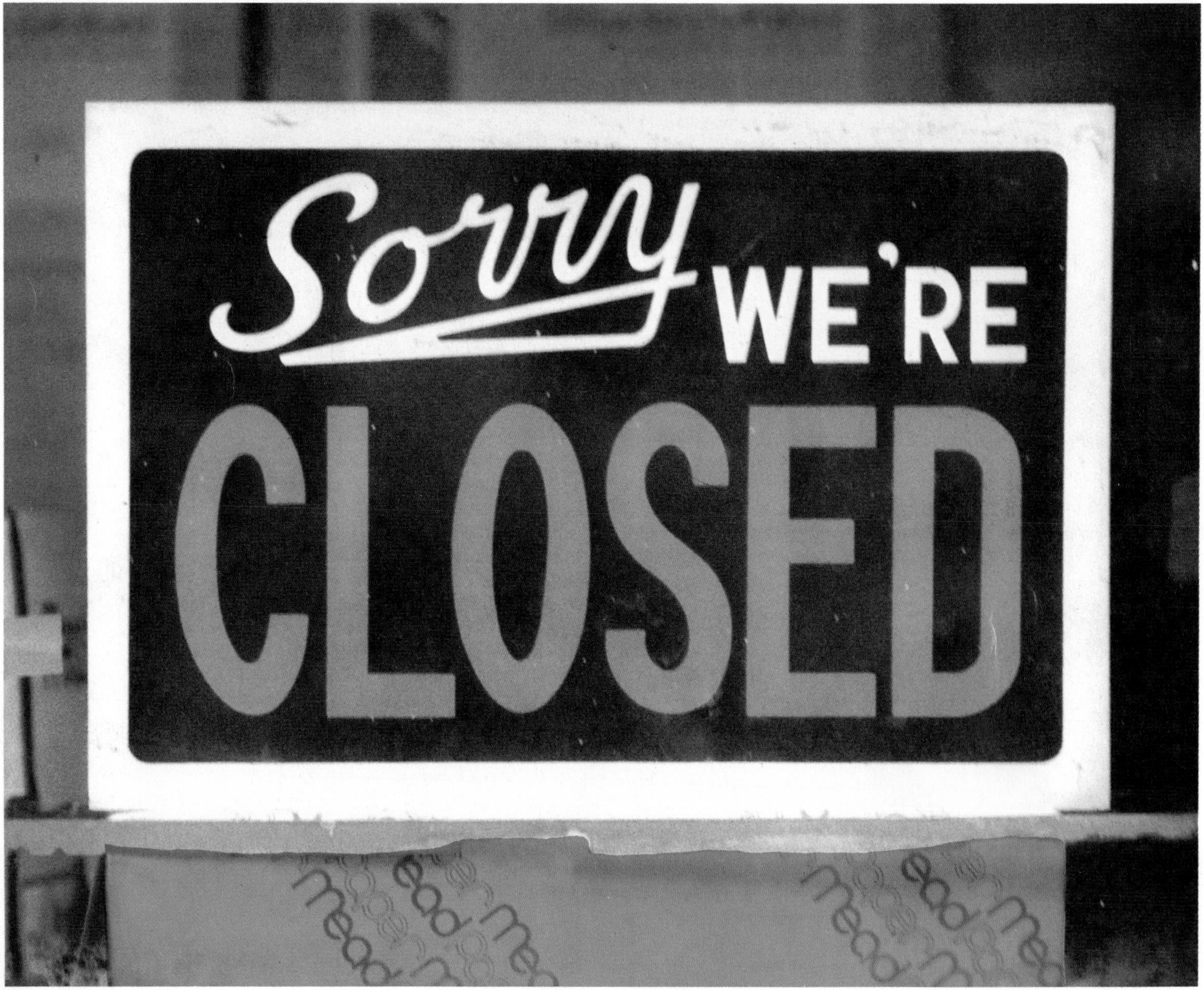
Sorry WE'RE
CLOSED

Amazing Makerspace

Fliers

PUBLIC LIBRARY DISTRICT OF COLUMBIA

KRISTINA A. HOLZWEISS

Children's Press®
An Imprint of Scholastic Inc.

Content Consultant
Shaunna Smith, EdD
Assistant Professor of Educational Technology
Department of Curriculum
Texas State University, San Marcos, Texas

Library of Congress Cataloging-in-Publication Data
Names: Holzweiss, Kristina A., author.
Title: Amazing makerspace DIY fliers / by Kristina Holzweiss.
Other titles: Amazing makerspace do-it-yourself fliers | True book.
Description: New York, NY : Children's Press, an imprint of Scholastic Inc., 2018. | Series: A true
   book | Includes bibliographical references and index.
Identifiers: LCCN 2017000976 | ISBN 9780531238462 (library binding) | ISBN 9780531240977 (pbk.)
Subjects: LCSH: Aeronautics—Juvenile literature. | Flight—Juvenile literature. | Handicraft—
   Juvenile literature.
Classification: LCC TL547 .H675 2018 | DDC 629.13—dc23
LC record available at https://lccn.loc.gov/2017000976

Front cover: Slingshot project

**Back cover: Student with Egg
Carton Helicopter project**

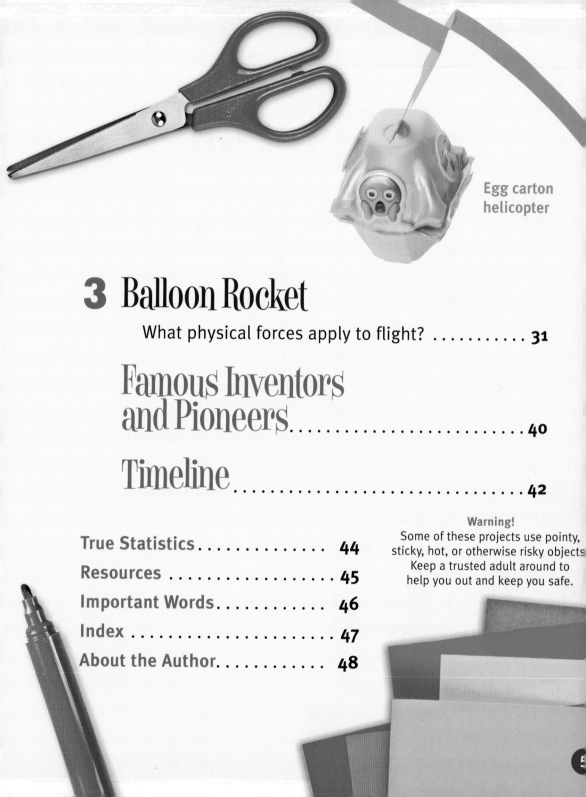

Egg carton
helicopter

Warning!
Some of these projects use pointy,
sticky, hot, or otherwise risky objects.
Keep a trusted adult around to
help you out and keep you safe.

You Can Be a Maker!

Makers are always thinking about problems and searching for ways to solve them. They create machines and test them out. Then they think about what they have learned and improve their work.

You can be a maker, too! This book will help you create objects that fly. After you follow the instructions to complete each project, you can experiment with your creations to make them even better.

Contents

THE **BIG** TRUTH!

Pioneers of Flight

Ready to fire
the slingshot

4

Find the Truth!

Everything you are about to read is true *except* for one of the sentences on this page.

Which one is **TRUE**?

T or F Helicopters and other aircraft rely on a force called lift to fly.

T or F There is only one type of energy.

Find the answers in this book.

Balloon Rocket

Slingshot

Egg Carton Helicopter

Think Ahead!

What does this helicopter have in common with certain types of seeds?

CHAPTER 1

Egg Carton Helicopter

Have you ever seen a helicopter flying through the sky? These incredible aircraft rely on spinning **rotors** to lift them into the air and steer them in the right direction. You can make a kind of helicopter in your own **makerspace**. In this project, you'll build a simple helicopter using supplies you may already have handy. You won't believe how easy it is to create your own simple flier.

You can see the first practical helicopter at the Henry Ford Museum.

Lifting Off

As a helicopter's rotors spin, they push down on the air beneath them. This creates a force called **lift** that pushes upward. This force is what allows the helicopter to rise into the air. With no engine or motor, your flier won't spin as quickly as the rotors on a real helicopter. As a result, it will create only enough lift to slow its fall. However, it will be able to float through the air for a short distance.

The purple arrow in this photo shows the movement of the rotor. The blue arrows shows how air moves over and under the blades of the rotor, creating lift.

The long parts of these seeds catch the air like the blades of a helicopter.

Seeds in the Wind

Some plants have seeds that work a lot like the helicopter you'll make in this project. When the wind blows these seeds off the plant, they start spinning. This provides lift, helping them float away from the plant before they land on the ground. As a result, new plants will be able to grow across a wider area and keep space between them.

Build a Helicopter

What You Need

- ⃝ **Scissors**
- ⃝ **Egg carton of any kind (cardboard, plastic, or foam)**
- ⃝ **Paper clip**
- ⃝ **Tape**
- ⃝ **Stickers, decorative tape, markers, crayons, or colored pencils**
- ⃝ **Sheet of cardstock that is 8.5 by 11 inches or larger**

Project Instructions

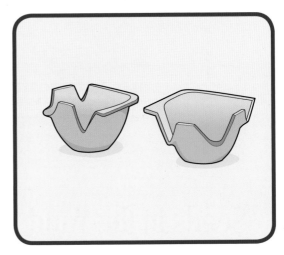

1. Use scissors to cut two cups out of an egg carton.

Unlike airplanes, helicopters can move straight up, down, backwards, and sideways.

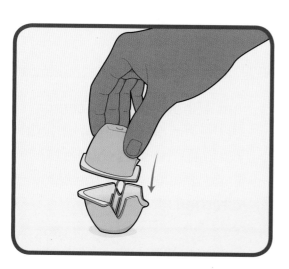

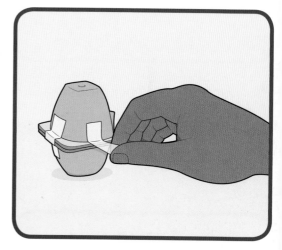

2. Set one cup on a flat surface. Place the paper clip inside. Set the other cup upside down on top of the first one so their edges meet.

3. Tape the two cups together. This will be the **cockpit** of your helicopter.

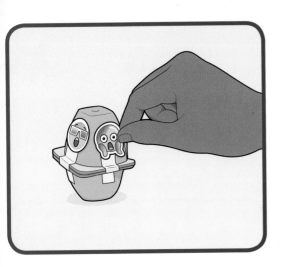

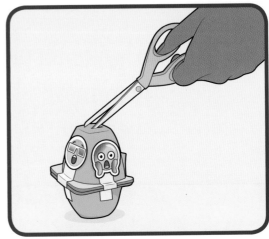

4. Decorate the cockpit using stickers, decorative tape, markers, colored pencils, or crayons.

5. Cut a short slit in the center of the top and bottom of your cockpit. The slits should be lined up and going the same direction.

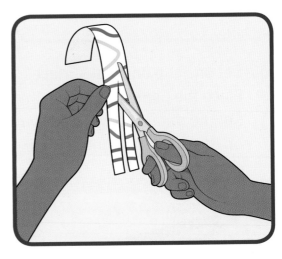

6. Cut a strip from the cardstock that is 11 inches (28 centimeters) long and 1 inch (2.5 cm) wide. Decorate it. This will be your helicopter's rotor.

7. Starting at one end of the strip, cut a slit 5.5 inches (14 cm) long down the middle. This forms the rotor's blades.

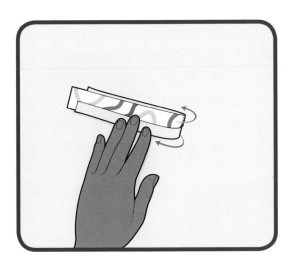

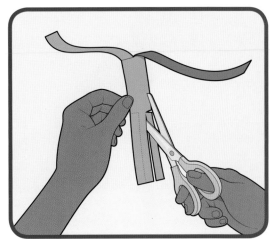

8. Fold the blades down so they stick out in opposite directions.

9. On the other end of the strip, opposite the rotor blades, trim the sides of the strip to make a tail narrow enough to fit in slits at the top and bottom of your cockpit.

10. Stick the tail through the slits in your cockpit. Tape it to the bottom of the cockpit.

1

Move It and Test It!

Stand up and drop the helicopter. Watch the helicopter spin! Can it carry the weight of the paper clip? Or does it go crashing to the ground? You might need to make some changes to the rotor. Now test how far it can travel. Place a yardstick on the ground and stand at the end of it. Toss the helicopter straight out in front of you, over the yardstick. How far does it travel?

Change It!

You can make your helicopter carry heavier **loads** or travel farther with some changes. Try building different versions of your helicopter.

- Use cardboard or other material for the rotors.
- Try three different types of egg carton for your cockpit: foam, cardboard, and plastic. Which performs best?
- Change the length of the rotor blades and tail and decorate them with colorful tapes.

How do you think each change will affect your helicopter's performance? Test each version. What differences do you notice? Why do you think those differences occur?

Think Ahead!
How does this slingshot launch the pompom ball?

About the Author

Kristina A. Holzweiss was selected by *School Library Journal* as the School Librarian of the Year in 2015. She is the founder of SLIME—Students of Long Island Maker Expo—and the president of Long Island LEADS, a nonprofit organization to promote STEAM education and the maker movement. In her free time, Kristina enjoys making memories with her husband, Mike, and their three children, Tyler, Riley, and Lexy.

Scholastic Library Publishing wants to especially thank Kristina A. Holzweiss, Bay Shore Middle School, and all the kids who worked as models in these books for their time and generosity.

PHOTOGRAPHS ©: 5 scissors and throughout: Marsel307/Dreamstime; 5 markers and throughout: photosync/Shutterstock; 5 bottom right: MNI/Shutterstock; 10: Spondylolithesis/Getty Images; 11: Flowerphotos/Eye Ubiquitous/Superstock, Inc.; 12 bottom: George Filyagin/Shutterstock; 12 graph paper and throughout: billnoll/iStockphoto; 17 right: Kryssia Campos/Getty Images; 17 left: Stockforliving/Shutterstock; 20: MihailUlianikov/iStockphoto; 21: Africa Studio/Shutterstock; 22 bottom left: james westman/Shutterstock; 27 left: ConstantinosZ/Shutterstock; 27 right: studiof22byricardorocha/iStockphoto; 28-29 background: Sunny Forest/Shutterstock; 28 bottom: Library of Congress; 29 top: akg-images/The Image Works; 29 bottom: Science and Society/Superstock, Inc.; 32: Aurora Open/Superstock, Inc.; 33: PhotoPierre/iStockphoto; 34 bottom left: byggarn.se/Shutterstock; 34 right: GooDween123/Shutterstock; 35 bottom: Yellowj/Shutterstock; 36 bottom: Alexander Tolstykh/Shutterstock; 37 bottom: Alexander Tolstykh/Shutterstock; 40 top left: Photo Researchers/Getty Images; 40 top right: Fine Art Images/Superstock, Inc.; 40 bottom: Photos.com/Thinkstock; 41 top left: Bob Thomas/Popperfoto/Getty Images; 41 top right: NYPL/Science Source/Getty Images; 41 bottom left: Bettmann/Getty Images; 41 bottom right: NASA/Superstock, Inc.; 42 top left: BnF, Dist. RMN-Grand Palais/Art Resource, NY; 42 top right: whitemay/iStockphoto; 42 bottom right: W.G. Jackman/D. Appleton & Co., New York/Library of Congress; 42 bottom left: Photo Researchers/Getty Images; 43 bottom center: Science Source; 43 bottom right: Fine Art Images/Superstock, Inc.; 43 top left: Bob Thomas/Popperfoto/Getty Images; 43 top right: NYPL/Science Source/Getty Images; 43 bottom left: Science and Society/Superstock, Inc.; 44: Spondylolithesis/Getty Images.

All instructional illustrations by Brown Bird Design.
All other images by Bianca Alexis Photography.

Index

Page numbers in **bold** indicate illustrations.

Important Words

airships (AIR-ships) inflated aircraft shaped like a sausage with engines and a passenger compartment hanging underneath

cockpit (KAHK-pit) the control area in an aircraft or boat where the pilot and sometimes the crew sit

drag (DRAG) the force that pushes against a moving object as the object moves forward

kinetic (ki-NET-ik) having to do with motion

lift (LIFT) the force that pushes upward on an object

loads (LOHDZ) objects that are being moved or carried

makerspace (MAY-kur-spays) any place where people plan, design, tinker, create, change, and fix things for fun or to solve problems

molecules (MAH-luh-kyoolz) the smallest units of a substance that still have all the properties of the substance and are composed of more than one atom

physics (FIZ-iks) the science that deals with matter and energy

rotors (ROH-turz) the blades of a helicopter that turn and lift the helicopter into the air

simple machine (SIM-puhl muh-SHEEN) a basic mechanical device for applying force

thrust (THRUHST) the force that pushes an object forward

Resources

Books

Gray, Susan Heinrichs. *Experiments With Motion*. New York: Children's Press, 2012.

Roslund, Samantha, and Emily Puckett Rodgers. *Makerspaces*. Ann Arbor, MI: Cherry Lake Publishing, 2014.

Wilkinson, Karen, and Mike Petrich. *The Art of Tinkering: Meet 150+ Makers Working at the Intersection of Art, Science, & Technology*. San Francisco: Weldon Owen, 2013.

Visit this Scholastic website for more information on fliers:
★ www.factsfornow.scholastic.com
Enter the keyword **Fliers**

True Statistics

Top speed of the North American X-15 rocket plane: 4,520 mph (7,274 kph)

Number of commercial airplane flights in the United States each day: About 23,911

Number of passengers who fly in the United States each year: About 900 million

Number of aircraft in the sky above the United States at any given time: About 7,000

Length of the Wright brothers' first successful flight: 120 ft (36.5 m) in 12 seconds

Did you find the truth?

T Helicopters and other aircraft rely on a force called lift to fly.

F There is only one type of energy.

Alberto Santos-Dumont completes the first airplane flight to be performed for the public in Europe.

Igor Sikorsky creates the first helicopter design to be mass-produced and widely used.

1903 **1906** **1927** **1942** **1961**

Pilot Charles Lindbergh makes the first-ever nonstop flight across the Atlantic Ocean.

Russian cosmonaut Yuri Gagarin becomes the first person to launch into outer space.

The Wright brothers make the first successful flight in a controlled, powered airplane.

Timeline

The first kites are flown in China.

The first hot-air balloon takes flight in France.

1000 BCE > **Late 1400s CE** > **1783** > **1839** >

Leonardo da Vinci creates designs for flying machines.

Charles Goodyear invents vulcanized rubber, making the first modern slingshots possible.

Alberto Santos-Dumont

(1873–1932) was a Brazilian innovator who worked on both airplanes and **airships**. In 1906, he made Europe's first airplane flight in his *14-bis*.

Igor Sikorsky

(1889–1972) was a Russian engineer who designed and built many aircraft. He is most famous for creating some of the earliest helicopters to come into widespread use.

Frank Whittle

(1907–1996) was an engineer in the English Royal Air Force who designed the first jet engines. This technology is used today to power most of the world's airplanes.

Wernher von Braun

(1912–1977) was a German engineer who made major advances in rocket technology. His designs helped the United States launch its first successful spacecraft.

Famous Inventors and Pioneers

Leonardo da Vinci

(1452–1519) was an Italian artist, inventor, and scientist who sketched many ideas for inventions in his notebooks. Among them were designs for aircraft and an early version of the parachute.

Galileo Galilei

(1564–1642) was an Italian scientist who made many important discoveries. His contributions to the field of physics have helped lead to many flight innovations.

Otto Lilienthal

(1848–1896) was a German inventor who became the first person to successfully build and fly gliders. Though he died during a flight in 1896, his work was a major inspiration to the Wright brothers and other innovators.

Change It!

You can alter the speed of your balloon rocket by making a few changes to your project. Try some of the ideas below. How do you expect each change would affect your rocket? Test out your creation. What differences do you notice? Why do you think those differences occur?

- Use a larger or smaller balloon.
- Use a different shape of balloon.
- Use a larger or smaller straw.
- Change the angle of the string so it tilts upward or downward.

Move It and Test It!

Now it is time to launch your rocket! Quickly remove the clothespin or clip and watch as the balloon zooms along the string. The balloon acts like a rocket. The air coming out of it creates thrust, which shoots the balloon forward. How far did the balloon go? Did it move quickly or slowly? ★

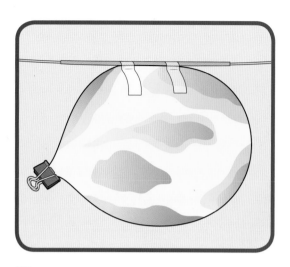

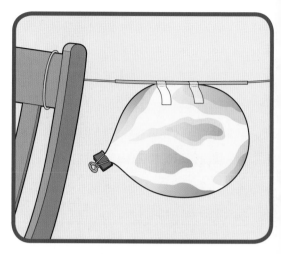

5. Tape the balloon to the bottom of the straw.

6. Slide the balloon and straw all the way to the end of the string. The balloon's opening should be pointing at the near end of the string.

You can also try tying the string to a doorknob or table leg.

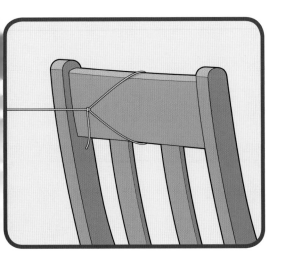

3. Tie the loose end of the string to the other chair and knot it. Make sure that the string is tight, straight, and level between the two chairs.

4. Blow up the balloon. Close the end with a clothespin or clip, but do not tie it.

Project Instructions

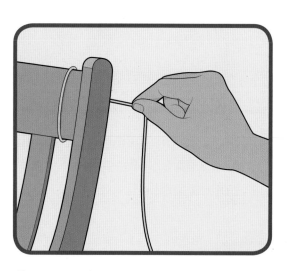

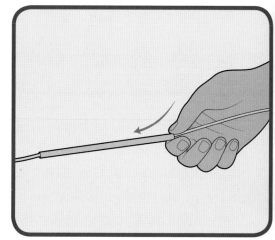

1. Tie one end of the string to a chair. Knot the string tightly.

2. Slide the loose end of the string through the straw.

Build a Balloon Rocket

What You Need

- [ ] 4 feet (1.2 meters) or more of string
- [ ] 2 chairs of equal height
- [ ] Drinking straw
- [ ] Balloon
- [ ] Clothespin or clip
- [ ] Tape

Before they were made of plastic, drinking straws were often made of wax-coated paper.

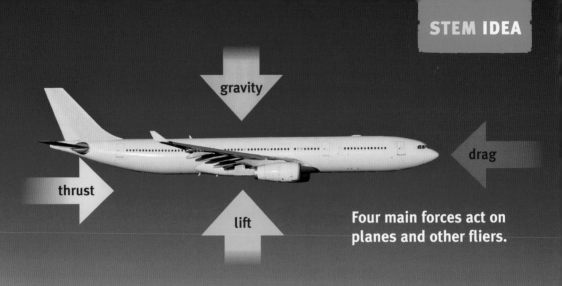

gravity

drag

thrust

lift

Four main forces act on planes and other fliers.

The Forces of Flight

An aircraft's engines create a force called **thrust** that pushes the aircraft through the air. This force is opposed by **drag**, which pushes against a flying object as it moves. As we discussed earlier, lift is a force that pushes an aircraft up. The force of gravity pulls a flying object down. To fly in the direction they want to go, pilots must make sure that all these forces are balanced correctly.

Action and Reaction

The third law of **physics** states that for every action, an equal reaction occurs in the opposite direction. This means that if you push an object, it also pushes back. As a rocket burns fuel, the air inside expands quickly and is forced out of the rocket. As the rocket pushes out the air, the air pushes back, moving the rocket forward.

As this hiker pushes against the boulder, an equal and opposite reaction pushes back.

CHAPTER 3

Balloon Rocket

Many flying objects, from spacecraft to missiles, rely on rockets to propel them through the air. These rockets are high-powered engines. They are very difficult to build on your own in a makerspace. However, you can use a balloon to see how rockets are able to push heavy vehicles into the air.

Scientist Michael Faraday created the first rubber balloon in 1824 for use in his experiments.

Think Ahead!

Which part of this flier acts like a rocket engine?

The brothers based their designs on existing gliders. They also took inspiration from the way birds hold their wings when gliding. The Wrights tested their first glider in 1900 in Kitty Hawk, North Carolina. They adjusted, tested, and improved their design over the next few years.

1900

Then, in 1903, the Wright brothers added an engine. On December 17, they made history by successfully taking to the sky in their powered airplane. The aircraft had room only for the pilot and had simple controls for steering. This airplane, making the first controlled, powered flight in history, changed the world forever.

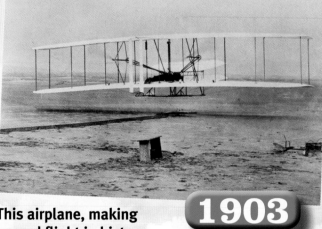

1903

Pioneers of Flight

Today, airplanes are a common sight. Thousands of planes take off from airports around the world every day. But that wasn't always the case. Before the 1900s, the closest invention to an airplane was a glider. Lacking an engine, a glider relies entirely on the wind for power and can fly only short distances.

1899

Brothers Orville and Wilbur Wright owned a successful bicycle shop in Dayton, Ohio. But their true passion was flying. In 1899, inspired by other aircraft inventors, they began working on their own gliders.

Change It!

You can change the design of your slingshot to adjust its power. Try some of the ideas below. How do you think each idea will change your slingshot? Test them out. What differences do you notice? Why do you think those differences occur?

- Use paper towel tubes to make your slingshot longer.
- Use smaller rubber bands.
- What else can you launch with your slingshot? Try cotton balls, crumpled up paper, or other soft loads.

Move It and Test It!

Find an open area. Load a pompom ball into the bigger tube so it rests on the end of the smaller tube. Pull the pencil back. Release it and watch the pompom fly! Now test your aim and the power of your slingshot. Stack a pyramid of paper or plastic cups on a table. How many shots does it take for you to knock them all down?

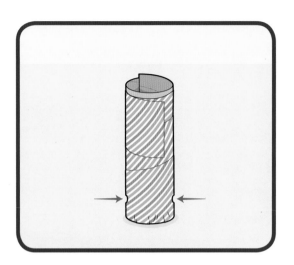

10. Punch another hole directly opposite the first at the same end of the tube.

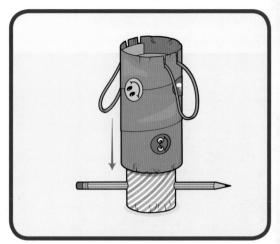

11. Push the pencil through the two holes. Slide the smaller tube into the larger tube. The larger tube will rest against the pencil.

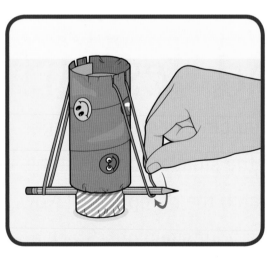

12. Hook the rubber bands around the ends of the pencil.

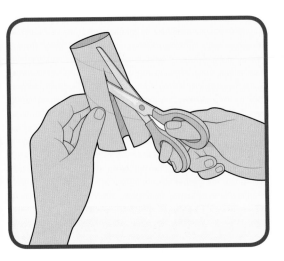

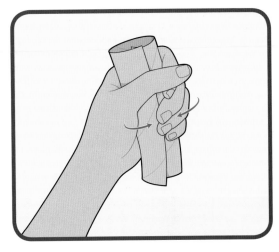

6. Cut along the entire length of the other toilet-paper tube.

7. Make the cut tube into a narrower cylinder by squeezing it. One cut end will be pushed inside the tube.

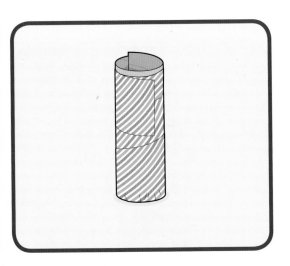

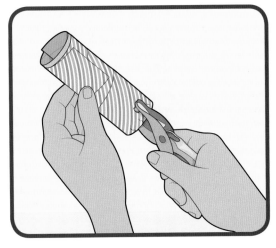

8. Tape around the shrunken tube with duct tape.

9. Using the hole punch, make one hole about 0.5 inch (1.3 cm) from the edge of the shrunken tube.

Project Instructions

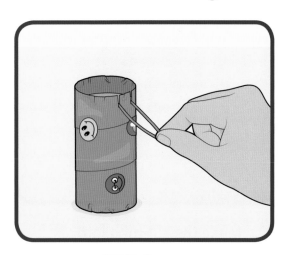

2. Decorate it using markers, stickers, or other supplies.

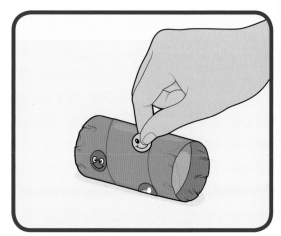

3. With scissors, cut two short slits about 0.5 inch (1.3 cm) apart into one end of the tube. Push a rubber band into the slits.

4. Cut two more slits directly opposite the others at the same end of the tube. Push the other rubber band into those slits.

5. Tape the ends of the rubber bands in place at the slits. Set this piece aside.

Build a Slingshot

What You Need

- ☐ **2 toilet-paper tubes**
- ☐ **Duct tape**
- ☐ **Markers, stickers, and other art supplies**
- ☐ **Scissors**
- ☐ **2 thin rubber bands**
- ☐ **Single-hole punch**
- ☐ **Pencil**
- ☐ **Large craft pompom balls**

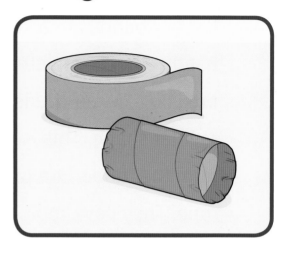

1. Reinforce one toilet-paper tube by wrapping it in duct tape.

U.S. astronauts have made many emergency repairs with duct tape.

What Makes Rubber Bands Stretchy?

Rubber bands are a key part of this project. These handy objects can stretch a long way before breaking. When you let go, they snap back to their regular shape. This is because the **molecules** that form the rubber are tangled together like a pile of rope. They have room to stretch out, but they are hard to break apart.

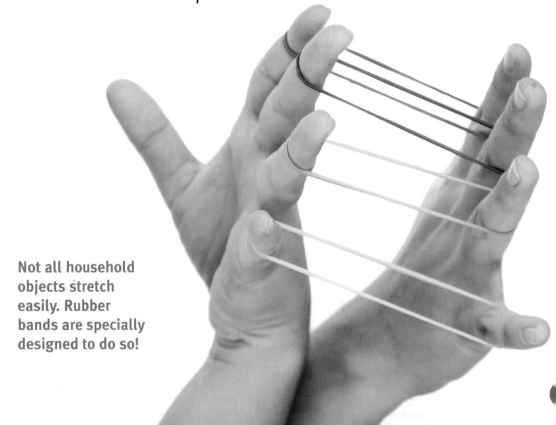

Not all household objects stretch easily. Rubber bands are specially designed to do so!

At this moment, kinetic energy is stored in the blue and red rubber bands of this slingshot.

Two Kinds of Energy

Like all simple machines, your slingshot relies on energy to do work. When you pull the slingshot back, it has potential energy. This means it has the ability to do something but hasn't done it yet. When you let go, the slingshot launches forward and shoots any load it is holding. This is called **kinetic** energy. Kinetic energy is energy in action!

CHAPTER 2

Slingshot

A slingshot is a kind of **simple machine**. Slingshots provide an easy way to launch objects through the air at high speed. However, they can be dangerous to use indoors or around people. In this project, you will build a slingshot that is safe to use anywhere—even in a crowded makerspace! You can use it to send pompom balls and other soft, lightweight objects zooming across the room.

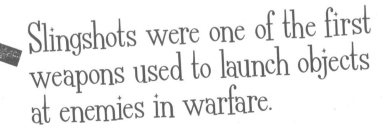

Slingshots were one of the first weapons used to launch objects at enemies in warfare.